W9-BEL-619

TO _____

FROM _____

A Challenge for Life

JAY STRACK

THOMAS NELSON PUBLISHERS
Nashville

Published in Nashville, Tennessee, by Thomas Nelson, Inc. and distributed in Canada by Lawson Falle, Ltd., Cambridge, Ontario.

Printed in the United States of America.

Library of Congress Cataloging-in-Publication Data
Strack, Jay.
  Aim high / Jay Strack.
    p. cm.
  ISBN 0-8407-7182-7
  1. Success—Religious aspects—Christianity. 2. Christian life—1960- I. Title.
BV4598.3.S77 1989
248.8'3—dc19
                                89-2958
                                   CIP

To Melissa Lynn, the love of my life:
Use your winsome spirit to aim high.

To Christina Diane, the light of my life:
Use your winning spirit to aim high.

I am proud of you both!

CONTENTS

1

THE MAN IN THE MIRROR

I am starting with the man in the mirror.
—*"Man in the Mirror"*
Sung by Michael Jackson

During these hectic weeks of graduation rites, which include parties, dates, baccalaureates, formals, and the ceremony itself, you have spent much time in front of the mirror. It is now time to reflect beyond just the physical and superficial. This is exactly what Michael Jackson suggests in his meaningful song of reflection on self and change.

When I was a teenager, the popular song that encouraged reflection was negative and destructive. John Lennon sang,

Imagine there's no heaven,
Imagine there's no hell.
Nothing to live or die for.

It was a generation of drop out and give up.

But today is a different day, and you are now facing the mirror to find your reflection.

Jackson makes some thought-provoking statements in his song "Man in the Mirror." He talks about deciding to his song "Man in the Mirror." He talks about deciding to make a difference in people's lives, to not ignore their needs, to stop being selfish and start reaching out. Try turning his thoughts into questions for yourself: Are you blind to needs because you pretend not to see? Is your love a selfish love? Do you want to change the world?

Jackson sings about making changes. He asks you to start with yourself. Give your love a home by helping someone in need. Make a difference in the world.

I don't know Michael Jackson's inspiration for this song, but his source could have been the most inspirational book in history, the Bible. Almost two thousand years ago, James instructed,

> Be doers of the word, and not hearers only, deceiving your-selves. For if anyone is a hearer of the word and not a doer, he is like a man observing his natural face in a mirror; for he observes himself, goes away, and immediately forgets what kind of man he was (James 1:22–24).

His words still apply today.

The ancient mirror of James was made of highly pol-ished metal. The modern mirror is made of glass. The materials may be very different, but both kinds of mirrors produce the same thing—a reflection of oneself. You must take the time to "observe" yourself.

The world today emphasizes observing others around you: the cars they drive, the clothes they wear, the way they act. Observing others can be a valuable learning experience, but the fact remains that the mirror reflects *you*, not anyone else. "Let a man examine himself" (1 Cor. 11:28), the Bible urges. Graduation is the time to ask your-self some personal questions and learn from the answers.

Who are you? Evaluate the person *you are*. "For most

who live, hell is never knowing who they are." This provocative statement is taken from the novel *The Singer.* Formal education often fails to prepare individuals to answer the basic questions of life. "Know thyself" or all other knowledge is incomplete. As Shakespeare said, "Of all knowledge, the wise and good seek most to know themselves."

To get to know who you really are, be honest with yourself. Remove the mask of who you want to be or who you pretend to be. The song "Masquerade" from the *Phantom of the Opera* tells of our ability to cover our true self with a false image: "Hide your face and the world will never find you." Many people hide from themselves. A hypocrite is a play actor, one who wears a mask; hypocrisy is hiding the truth from yourself.

Come out from behind the veil and realistically take inventory of your strengths and weaknesses. In business and financial statements, these are called assets and liabilities. *Your best asset is that you are the crowning act of God's direct creation.*

Your body was formed in a way similar to the way a master artist forms a sculpture. You may quickly think, *I wish my sculpture was a little more sculpted!* There are steps you can take to change your body, and there are things about your body you can never change. That's the way God planned it!

God also created your mind. He provided you with the potential to readily store information, learn new facts, and understand mysteries. Remember, God is not responsible for your grades or the way that you use your mind. He offers it to you for development and use. Each person's mind learns, stores, and understands in a way that is unique to him alone.

This uniqueness results in what we call strengths and weaknesses. Most people are quick to observe their faults without giving themselves credit for their strengths. Write down all of your good qualities you can think of. Ask friends and family to help. Perhaps you are kind and caring and willing to help others. Or you may have good leadership or listening skills. Maybe you excel in special hobbies. Or you may have the ability to make friends easily. Perhaps you have a way of making others smile because you are always exuding happiness. That's a wonderful gift. No asset is too small. After all, God put each one inside you.

A healthy self-image is essential. You cannot consistently perform in a manner that is not agreeable with how you see yourself.

When I looked in the mirror on the eve of my graduation, I was not proud of the person I had been. Because of my abuse of drugs and alcohol, I had literally wasted my high school experience. My grades were barely above failing because I simply had not applied myself. I was short on relationship skills because I was living only for myself. That night I made up my mind that I would no longer be the same person.

With Christ in my life, I determined to "put off the old and put on the new." Not only did I pursue a college education, but I graduated *cum laude* in two years rather than four. This *D* and *F* student in high school worked through a master's program and then obtained a Doctor of Ministries degree. I am the author of five books. How did such a change take place? My motivation came from these words: "One thing I do, forgetting those things which are behind and reaching forward to those things which are ahead, I press toward the goal for the prize of the upward call of God in Christ Jesus" (Phil. 3:13,14). I believed that God had a plan for my life, and I set about to work at following it.

Once you have looked at the person you are right now, begin to plan the person you want to be. If the two seem far apart, don't be discouraged. Life is just beginning, and change can occur.

My friend Zig Ziglar tells his audiences, "It's not where you start, but where you finish." I have come to realize that each tomorrow is a chance to improve, to set a wrong right, to grow closer to the person I want to be and God wants me to be.

Moving closer to your goal as a person will happen only through having and following a clear direction. So, where are you going in life? You are going in the direction you are now headed! Whether you are like a ship caught in the storm, tossed about by every change of wind and tide, no particular course charted, whether you are sailing on a smooth sea paying careful attention to the compass with a definite port and arrival time, or whether you are somewhere in between will determine when and how you change to a person you like and feel comfortable being.

Some key questions on this lifetime journey include the following: Am I really content to live the rest of my life as I am right now? What do I want out of life? What did God have in mind when He created me?

Whatever you have or have not accomplished until now is not what you determine your success by. You cannot be discouraged about yesterday any more than you can wait on tomorrow. You must begin the process of change today.

There are four basic types of people:

1. *Wishers*. These people try to wish things into being. They go through life wishing and hoping things will hap-

pen for or to them. They say things like, "I wish I had a new car, I wish I was popular, I wish I had more money or more education."

Wishers are still reciting the poem "Star light, star bright, first star I see tonight, I wish I may, I wish I might, have this wish I wish tonight." These individuals will never change until they *stop wishing* on a star and *start reaching* for the stars.

2. *Complainers*. Complainers are never happy. You know them. No matter what happens, it's always someone else's fault: "Mom always did like her best. It's not fair. She always gets the lucky break." Nothing seems to satisfy, and nothing is easy enough. These pessimists see only the bad side of circumstances and never even think to look for a solution or accept the challenge.

3. *Sleepwalkers*. These people simply don't know what's happening. They have dropped out of life through using alcohol and/or drugs or have escaped reality in other ways. Life is too difficult, they have decided. And so, it's back to bed to hide under the covers. Sleepwalkers are content to let events go on around them while they barely get by.

4. *Doers*. Doers take action. People in this group make things happen through hard work. This is the group God had in mind when He created human beings in His own image. The other groups are "hearers" only, and they deceive themselves.

Being a part of one of these groups can be temporary. In *Top Performance*, Zig Ziglar reminds us, "You are what you are and where you are because of what has gone into your mind; you change what you are and where you are by changing what goes into your mind."

Decide to take charge of the feeding of your mind by carefully selecting what you allow to go into it. You are the only person on earth who can control the input into your mind. Some types of influence are uncontrollable—the news you hear, the everyday facts of crime and bad news, the negative attitudes flung at you on the job or at school. Other, more powerful brain input *can* be controlled: good music, Scripture memory, positive friends and acquaintances, and of course, the reading of good books.

2

AIM HIGH

I SAM. 17:4-11
      32-37
      38-51

To aim is to strive toward a specific target or goal. When you shoot an arrow, you must aim or you hit nothing. Too many grads are just pointing the arrow and letting it fly, and it just falls to the ground.

It is much easier to barely get by, to go through the motions, than it is to set a goal and work toward it. On the other hand, you might be working very hard, but never actually achieving a purpose. Why? Because you have set no definite goals to accomplish.

Sometimes people are afraid to set goals because of past experiences. You may have had a target and then missed it. As a result, you lowered your standard to a goal that required little or no effort.

But God's plan for life indicates that getting by is not enough for us. John 10:10 says that Jesus came that we might have abundant life—life that is full and overflowing with purpose. Our standard is for excellence, not just good. We are to succeed, not just survive. Beware of the enemy of mediocrity and begin to view each failure as another rung on the ladder toward success. Excellence must be cultivated, but the melody of mediocrity seems to be deafening too many graduates' ears.

I'm not suggesting that you follow a course of blind

ambition. All of us have various strengths and weak-nesses, but the key is this: *all of us do have strengths*. Use yours to reach for the moon, and if you don't make it, you'll still have grabbed a few stars along the way.

One young man overcame all the odds, brushed aside fear, and faced the challenge. David took the challenge when everyone was against him: family—his brothers laughed; friends—the army teased him; foe—Goliath mocked him. He believed he could do it. If he had taken the easy way out, David still would have been a "good kid," but he would have missed the chance to conquer the apparently impossible.

How did David, a small shepherd boy, defeat Goliath, the Philistine giant? With a sense of purpose and sin-gleness of mind, he prepared for battle. He took with him five smooth stones. Also included in his ammunition to win the battle and complete the vision, the goals he had set before himself, were:

G od-given vision.

O rganize or agonize.

A ssess strengths and weaknesses.

L earn to lean on God.

S ee obstacles as opportunities.

1. *David had God-given vision.* He had a vision of win-ning. He set a goal, a target. Two options were available to him: tackle the insurmountable object or let it tackle him. He took the initiative and met the challenge: "David hastened and ran toward the army to meet the Philistine" (1 Sam. 17:48).

2. *David organized a plan* of action to defeat the giant. He

17

identified what was required to conquer Goliath—perfect aim and courage—and he determined the enemy's weakness, which was overconfidence. While Goliath mocked the boy's size (1 Sam. 17:42,43), David saw his chance. As the giant lowered his guard, the young boy aimed his stone into the one unprotected area of Goliath's body that would kill him instantly.

3. *David assessed his strengths and his weaknesses.* His weakness was obvious—he was just too small to have enough strength to win over a giant. But that didn't stop him. He just had to find another way. His strength *seemed* small—he had been protecting sheep from lions and bears with a slingshot. However, his aim was perfect! He had continually practiced hitting the mark as a young shepherd boy (1 Sam. 17:34–36).

4. *David learned to lean on God* to help him achieve his goal of destroying Goliath. He did not allow the circumstances to control him. He informed the king of his people, Saul, that God, who had delivered him from life's daily pitfalls, would continue to do so now (1 Sam. 17:37). Then David addressed Goliath "in the name of the LORD of hosts" (1 Sam. 17:45). "The battle is the LORD's," he cried, "and He will give you into our hands" (1 Sam. 17:47).

5. *David could see obstacles as opportunities.* "What shall be done for the man who kills this Philistine?" he asked (1 Sam. 17:26). While others feared Goliath, David thought of him in terms of a trophy for the people and for his God. He knew the rewards were great and had decided it was worth the risk to win. *Some said the giant was too big to hit; David claimed he was too big to miss!*

How do *you* slay a giant? You will always live in a world of seemingly impossible hurdles. There will always be situations in your life that appear utterly futile. There will always be plenty of Goliaths. But like David, you have a choice. Either you beat them, or they beat you.

Carefully select your stones. Ready your sling shot. Look your giants in the eyes, then aim high—aim to win. Concentrate on your vision of winning until it becomes a reality. Strive for the qualities of a winner—dreams, direction, and determination.

Will you be a voice or an echo? Make up your mind now and declare, "I will not repeat what the crowd says and does. I will not let circumstances determine my life." The cry of a person aiming high is "I will be a voice."

A winner is extremely careful of whose guidelines she follows. She aligns her standards with the standards of God and does not detour along with the crowd.

Setting goals is only the beginning. You may set goals and have great ideas, but seldom see them become reality. The negative influences in the world may be so over-powering that you succumb to them. People are quick to say that "it can't be done," that your past track record is full of failures, that they tried it and it didn't work. The news-papers headline the bad news: who cheated, what's wrong with the world, why people can't win.

Don't give in to such negativism. Surround yourself with winners and encouragers. Read about people who *do* live moral lives and who *are* changing the world; find out about the great advancements and achievements man *is* capable of. The best-seller book list always contains sever-al biographies of winners, people who have defied the odds. These are inspiring and challenging. They keep you aiming ever higher, as God planned for you to do.

Your attitude is everything. Without a positive attitude, you have nowhere to go (or grow). In Philippians 4:8 Paul says to think on and contemplate the good things, the pure things, in life. By doing this, you can develop and maintain a positive attitude to help you toward your goals.

Once you aim high, your enthusiasm builds toward the mark. Yet enthusiasm can leave as quickly as it came. Yesterday may have been wonderful, but today brings many problems. You must go to the source of enthusiasm so that the well will never run dry. You can manufacture only so much enthusiasm without depleting yourself, but God is the fountain that springs forth eternally. *Enthusiasm* is literally *en theos* ("in God"), and it is an overflow He causes to come from within you.

The joy from within is obtained, first, by coming to know Christ personally, and second, by developing that relationship of trust and love with Him. The Bible is His love letter to us through which each of us is encouraged, corrected, instructed, and challenged.

You've been challenged before, you've been enthused before, but what lies between the setting of the goal and the reaching of the goal? What is the obstacle that keeps you from accomplishing what you set out to do? Dreams perish, ideas die out, and the drive for excellence is replaced with just getting by when you lose the vision you once believed in.

Let's go back to David's formula G O A L S:

G od-given vision.

O rganize or agonize.

A ssess strengths and weaknesses.

L earn to lean on God.

S ee obstacles as opportunities.

1. God-given vision. Dare to be different, to dream a dream! You were engineered and designed by your Creator for success. You were created in God's image with great potential to rule and to reign over the earth. He longs for you to aim high and to allow Him to be your source of motivation.

The vision to compete and win must be more than an idea; it must dominate your mind. Never say, "I might," "I'll try," or "I'll give it a shot." Always state, "I will," "I can," "I must." The writer of Proverbs observed that "where there is no vision, the people perish" (29:18, KJV). Don't perish—pulsate with life fueled by a God-given vision.

2. Organize or agonize. Most dreams die at this stage. The goals are never filled with life-giving breath. Instead they die on the "wish list." It pays to write down your goal. Set a date. Organize at the outset to avoid disappointments later.

Never be afraid to ask for help. Most successful people are more than happy to assist you, for they themselves were once (and probably will be again) on the asking side. Make a list of contact people who can help you achieve your goal.

Next, identify the stages of your plan. Within the long-term goal will be short-term goals or "steps" toward the end result.

For example, let's say your goal is to become a well-known lecturer on foreign affairs. You might develop an outline like this:

A. I need the following education: (name it). Decide on what kind of degree and which college. Consider what alternative types of education (seminars, lectures, tc.) may help. Give a completion target date for each.

B. This year I will volunteer at a politician's office.

C. Next year I will obtain a job doing behind-the-scenes work.

D. I will attend (number) lectures of various speakers to learn technique and gather information.

E. I will begin speaking at clubs and organizations that I am involved in by (date).

F. I will broaden my contacts and friends.

G. I will devise a plan for keeping my information current.

H. Because of reaching the above goals, I will be lecturing on foreign affairs in (number) years.

Unless each of the short-term goals is completed, you will never realize your vision. Impose time limits on yourself, but only allow them to motivate you, never to discourage you.

3. Assess strengths and weaknesses. More often than not, weaknesses become assets when closely examined. Simply not knowing how to do something is not a weakness; it is a challenge! Determine the needed levels of skills and knowledge. If you already have them, great! Build on them. If you don't, great! Begin immediately to attain them through learning and growing. (The two always go together.)

Author Denis Waitley stresses that there is an immense difference between limits and limitations. There are certain physical limits in life: if you are five eight, you probably will not play in the NBA; if you are under the age of thirty-five, it is illegal for you to run for the presidency of the United States. And there are mental limits: you may not have the mental capacity or inclination to be a physicist or a nuclear scientist. You do, however, have some of every quality it takes to be a success in some area.

Be realistic in your assessment. Limits are physical or material: the amount of money you have, where you live, who you know. Sometimes these can be changed or compensated for; other times they remain to be used as guidelines.

Limitations, on the other hand, are usually self-imposed. These include lack of organization, motivation, and systems of goal setting and achieving. Deal with these at the beginning of your evaluation.

4. Learn to lean on God. The apostle Paul learned how to do this, and he said, "I can do all things through Christ who strengthens me" (Phil. 4:13). You can too. No matter how much you lack, no matter how much you have, God planned it all. He is the source you can rely on: "For with God nothing will be impossible" (Luke 1:37).

In the introduction to his commentary on the book of Romans, Martin Luther defined *faith* as "a living and daring confidence in God's grace, so sure and certain that a man would stake his life on it 1,000 times." You can certainly stake your future and your life on God and His help.

Pray as though it all depends on God; work as though it all depends on you. His desire is for you to conquer life and enjoy it. He is the best business partner you will ever confide in!

5. See obstacles as opportunities. For every reason why

you think you can't, generate reasons why you *must*. Keep the reward in mind as well as the goal. Through the difficulties, look ahead to the joy in the result. "No pain, no gain" is more than just a saying for athletes.

Even the greatest obstacles can be opportunities. I overcame a life of drug addiction and used what I learned through the experience to become the author of *Drugs and Drinking: What Every Parent and Teen Should Know* as well as a speaker to over four million students about drug abuse. As a teen, I hid my insecurities by being the class clown. Now I can effectively motivate people with my sense of humor.

Yes, it's easier to crawl in bed and pull the covers up over your head than to face all your responsibilities and challenges. Graduation is scary, but it's also exciting! You have more potential than you realize. Make the most of what you have and live life to the fullest as God intends for you to do. Learn to think in terms of maximizing the opportunities and minimizing the obstacles.

If you never aim, you'll never hit the target. If you're content to be bored, to let life pass you by, you will never really know just how much you can do. The world is yours, new grad. Say "Yes!" to being your best, to the willingness to go the extra mile in all that you do. Trusting in God, you can conquer the world as you *aim high*!

3

FUTURE SHOCK

Future Shock is a term borrowed from Alvin Toffler, author of the best-selling book by the same name. It describes how the average high-school senior feels as he faces graduation—so overwhelmed with the unknown, the fear of being alone, going off to college, leaving behind family and friends. Just thinking of it can cause the new grad to break into a cold sweat.

Man was made to look toward adventure, to an emerging brave new world. He was created to walk upright so that he might look forward and upward. Don't worry about the trip down the unknown path. You may feel like Captain Kirk of "Star Trek" fame—going where no man has gone before! Rest assured: God has gone before you to plan your future, and if you watch carefully for the signs, His road map will carry you through to college, a career, and beyond.

Although change can be frightening, the more control you exercise over your circumstances, the less impact future shock will have on you. Dr. Tim LaHaye writes that the future belongs to those who prepare for it spiritually, educationally, relationally, and vocationally. I hasten to add *effectively*, for all of the others can be of no merit if carried out haphazardly.

These can be visualized through the acrostic SERVE:

S piritually

E ducationally

R elationally

V ocationally

E ffectively

Spiritually

Spiritual growth depends on personal holiness. Holiness is to be a vital part of every believer's life rather than of the lives of the exceptional few. Since the word *holy* is found in different forms six hundred times throughout the Bible, the biblical authors apparently recognized the quality as a significant one for their readers.

To be holy is to turn from sin and self and seek conformity to the nature of God. Ephesians 5:1 admonishes us to be "followers of God as dear children," literally, to "keep on becoming imitators of God."

The power of the Holy Spirit, the prayer of faith, the study of the Word of God, and obedience to God's will—all combine to give each of us the strength to undertake the work of holiness.

By God's grace, you are enabled to adopt a lifestyle of holiness, that is, obedience to the will of God. As you show your desire to be holy by guarding your mind and emotions, controlling your appetites and desires, you develop holy habits that will remain with you as you grow.

Educationally

If you are undecided about going to college, consider the fact that most companies continue to train and retrain employees throughout their working years. Education is not simply related to a prescribed number of years in college; it is a constant process of change. In today's high-tech world, vocational and technical schools may be the option you are looking for.

One very promising possibility is to enlist in the military. Not only is your education paid for, but you earn a salary while you learn. The discipline and the determination you can gain are valuable in building a successful life. Patriotism is one of America's greatest strengths, and belonging to our military brings with it honor and prestige.

Whichever road you choose, understand that education in today's world is vital. It is no longer an option; it is an absolute.

While you are deciding on a career, cover the basics before you start specializing. Even if you are sure of your career path, other aspects of an occupation may open in the future for which you will need these skills. For example, basic business skills are needed in every career, from engineering to advertising, ministry to public relations, scientific research to retail.

Of course, computers abound now in every business, including service stations, factories, retail shops, law firms, medical facilities, engineering firms, you name it! They are no longer limited to accounting or banking.

Megatrends author John Naisbitt illustrates their importance:

In the new information society, being without computer skills is like wandering around a collection the size of the Library of Congress with all the books arranged at random with no Dewey Decimal system, no card catalogue—and of course no friendly librarian to serve your information needs.

Many colleges are requiring graduates to demonstrate the ability to write a simple computer program.

Computer training is an imperative as is math. A second language is also becoming expected more and more frequently in the workplace, with Spanish now being second only to English in the world.

It has been said that to be really successful, you will have to be trilingual: fluent in English, Spanish, and computer. I would add one more and make it quadlingual; you should also be fluent in knowledge of the Bible. The Bible is the mouthpiece of God, what He uses to communicate Himself to us; and through us and our knowledge of the Bible, He can communicate to those who do not know Him. The Word is our "road map" for what lies ahead, and without it we do not have direction.

If you choose to attend college, don't panic if you are unresolved about your major. You have the security of taking two years of basic course requirements before you have to decide.

James 1:5 directs us to ask God for wisdom, for He gives it liberally. Seek advice, but take care that it is godly advice. The view of the world can be so much different from God's plan for your life. And His is always the best for you, as Romans 8:28 says: "We know that all things work together for good to those who love God, to those who are the called according to His purpose."

Relationally

Relationships also enter a new phase for the graduate. Friendships deepen and find new meaning, and dating becomes more serious. Friendships and intimate relationships play an enormous part in the well-being of the total person.

All of us have felt the emptiness resulting from conflict with a loved one. As Christians, we are responsible to heal the hurt by taking the initiative in forgiving and asking forgiveness. Don't let pride interfere with a joyful relationship. It only leads to problems in other areas. A friend who forgives and loves is a good friend. Select your friends carefully, realizing that you will become more and more like each other.

The growing of friendships is vital training for marriage. Learning to forgive is imperative for a marriage to succeed. Accepting a spouse unconditionally is what God asks of us. If you cannot accept a friend on these terms, then you will have difficulty accepting a spouse on similar terms.

For these reasons you can understand the importance of choosing Christian friends of both sexes whose moral values parallel your own. This doesn't mean that you should never reach out to a person who doesn't know Christ. On the contrary, adopt a lifestyle of reaching out and caring, but allow "Christ in you" (Col. 1:27) to do the influencing instead of permitting yourself to be influenced by non-Christians.

The same is true in so-called missionary dating—going out with someone for the purpose of bringing them to Christ. This concept of dating has many drawbacks. Think about where you are going and what you are going to do or see. Are you being dated because your lifestyle is an example, or are you being asked to compromise your convictions? Invite your unsaved friends to join in activities in your church or to go on a double or group date with Christian friends. Then you will be safer from a bad reputation and alluring temptations.

Never date anyone you would not marry! This advice may sound extreme, but consider what it means. Even if you start out as just friends having fun, you could end up being very attracted to each other. This is especially true of Christians dating non-Christians. In fact, 90 percent of all marriage problems were produced by improper dating. And many of those abused by a spouse had sexual relations with that individual before marriage. Others simply married the wrong person because of a strong physical attraction.

Friendship is an essential part of life. Take the time to cultivate friendships by being a friend—listening, caring, helping, encouraging, and praying. In friendship, as in life, you reap what you sow. You will find more joy and contentment in giving than in receiving. A one-sided friendship is short-lived.

Ask God to supply you with Christian friends. Don't constantly bombard yourself with temptation by being with the "wrong" crowd.

F orgive and be forgiven.

R eap what you sow.

I gnore temptations from peers.

E xpand opportunities to meet new friends.

N ecessary part of life.

D ate in God's will.

Vocationally

Choosing a career that you enjoy is important because you will spend the majority of your life learning about and building your career. Too many times young people choose a career based on how much money they expect to make. They have chosen the lifestyle they desire and try to match the income to it. The end result is that life runs them instead of their mastering it. The quest for excellence is replaced by a drive for materialism, and that drive is one that can never satisfy.

For many people, money becomes a god to serve, to worship with careful devotion. Evil is born out of the prominent role money plays when it interferes with the willingness to obey God and interrupts a time of service for Him: "For the love of money is a root of all kinds of evil, for which some have strayed from the faith in their greediness, and pierced themselves through with many sorrows" (1 Tim. 6:10). Notice the word that is so often ignored—*love*. Money is not in itself evil, but the love of money is.

Examine your priorities. Be courageous enough to live simply in order to do what you want to do and what God has shown you. Don't begin now to give in to peer pressure. Pray about God's will for your life. When God is in control of your life, the money to which He leads you will most certainly be enough. And when your career is on track, your marriage, your friendships, and your happiness will be the better for it.

The pressures of family members and their expectations may be confusing your decisions. They may be unwilling to let you develop a new area, particularly one that will take a long time to build into a self-supporting career. Can you show them that you are willing to wait on success and support yourself in other ways in the intervening time? If you're serious about making it on your own, begin now to set up a budget, including savings, and work toward achieving that goal.

Be flexible! Be open to changes in the direction of your life. Be willing to start at the bottom and "learn" your way up. For example, the manager of a hotel must understand the job of every employee—from those in housekeeping to security to the restaurant, the front desk, the office, and everyone in between. Of course, a college education will prepare her, but she must have hands-on experience to really understand the business. The same is true for a restaurant, travel agency, retail store, or other businesses. Many college graduates want top executive and managerial positions from the moment they get their degrees. Why not start out during college in the field you want to be ready to "move up in" instead of "moving in" after graduation?

Use your summers and/or part-time work to test the waters of the field you are dreaming of or leaning toward. For example, if you are interested in law, take a job as a "runner"; that is, one who does legal research, runs errands, and so on. If you are interested in medicine, be a volunteer in a hospital. A would-be pastor can learn a great deal by working with a youth group or a Sunday school class. A future Certified Public Accountant (CPA) can begin with simple bookkeeping and the checking of figures. The opportunities to "try before you buy" are limited only by your imagination.

Whatever field you choose, be prepared to work—and to work hard. Take pride in your daily efforts: "Whatever you do in word or deed, do all in the name of the Lord Jesus" (Col. 3:17). God honors the giving of your best.

Once you have a job, you will want to guard your testimony as a Christian, but don't worry about making mistakes. If you blow it—either in labor or in emotion—you can correct it. If you go through your days as a perfect person, you'll hardly be noticed, but make a mistake and the whole world looks on! The way you handle that mistake is what others will remember about you. Never be too proud to apologize, whether you were at fault or not. Never be too proud to learn from an error in judgment.

It is quite probable that more of your coworkers will be non-Christians than Christians. You must never set aside your principles, even for a moment. You must determine in your heart that you will influence others in morality, rather than be influenced, before the temptation ever arises. Your attitude and workmanship may be the only reflection of Jesus they ever see.

Effectively

To proceed effectively in the areas discussed, you must have a sure foundation in each. You cannot build the walls or the roof or even put in a floor of a home until the foundation is stable.

Spiritually, you cannot build until you are sure of a personal relationship with Christ.

Educationally, you cannot build until you have done your best on the course you are studying *right now.*

Relationally, you cannot build until your current relationships are growing and important to you.

Vocationally, you cannot build until you are willing to work your hardest at whatever opportunity is before you.

Change is inevitable. Meet it head-on. Yes, the world looks frightening. Newspaper headlines declare dangerous days:

"U.S. Accuses Soviets of Violation of Missile Treaty"

"Violence Heats Up on the West Bank"

"Stock Market Crashes to Lowest This Year"

"Job Outlook Bleak for New Graduates"

These are scary, indeed. It makes one wonder if it's even worth trying, if success is ever possible. *Except for one thing I forgot to mention.* These headlines are from the year *I* graduated: 1971! Some things never change.

4

CHOICES, CHOICES, CHOICES

Having to make decisions on your own is probably a new frontier. "On your own" may mean without parents, but it does not mean without God. You can have confidence in the One who cleanses you of your past, makes sense of your present, and holds your future in His hands.

Many factors hinder decision making. One of the most obvious is worry. It clouds the mind and distorts the thinking. It becomes an obsession and destroys an individual's joy and peace.

Unfortunately, worry is a way of life for too many people. The word comes from an Old English term, which means "to strangle." Worrying can actually strangle you mentally, physically, and spiritually. It can literally choke the life out of your future.

With this in mind, you can grasp the meaning of Paul's words in Philippians 4:6: "Be anxious for nothing, but in everything by prayer and supplication, with thanksgiving, let your requests be made known to God." *To be anxious* is "to be torn apart." To cleanse your mind of worry, *redirect your thinking.*

People are destroyed by worry when the thoughts in the mind affect the feelings in the heart. Wrong thinking causes wrong feelings. And these feelings feed the mind, resulting in a vicious cycle.

Time to sort out your feelings is a luxury you may not have in today's fast-paced world. Upon graduation you begin the most drastic change since fighting your way out of the womb. (You did that so well, you were probably spanked.) Few grads understand that your generation must adjust to the most rapid pace of change in history. A new set of decisions is likely to face you daily.

When you are uncertain in your decisions, you will be fearful of accepting responsibility, of facing the unknown.

Early in my college days, I had a professor who was sensitive to the fear his students felt of the unknown, of this new world where so much was expected of them. One day in class, he closed his book and taught us how to face that fear. I have never forgotten his formula:

F E A R = **F** alse

E vidence that

A ppears

R eal

He then had us memorize the verse: "God has not given us a spirit of fear, but of power, and of love, and of a sound mind" (2 Tim. 1:7).

Fear of facing the unknown future, of accepting responsibility, or of failing is remedied by having faith in the living God who cares for you. Fear has no cure other than choosing to *aim high* while trusting in God. So what if you fail today? Tomorrow is a clean slate. You can always start over, but not until you start the first time!

Many a championship boxing match has been won in the last round. A *good* boxer gives it all he's got from the first round. A *great* boxer continues to get up for the tenth round when he's been knocked down the other nine rounds.

Worry and fear are so closely related, they might be called cousins. Neither can change the outcome of your life, unless you allow one or both of them to keep you from aiming high, from making clear decisions.

Today's choices determine your tomorrow, the outcome of your success. Mary Kay Ash says, "Be careful of the choices you make today. They will become your lifestyle tomorrow."

Today's choices have consequences for today and responsibility for eternity. Matthew 12:36 records these words of Jesus: "But I say to you that for every idle word men may speak, they will give account of it in the day of judgment."

The decisions you make today set the course of your life. When then vice-presidential candidate Daniel Quayle made the statement, "I did not know in 1969 that I would be in this room today," he was explaining the decision he had made to enlist in the National Guard rather than serve in regular military service. At the time, he was eighteen, just out of high school, and it didn't really seem to matter. But twenty years later, it did matter as his past record was scrutinized by the public. They wanted to know if this man could make proper choices before they would cast a vote in his favor.

Every person's actions are recorded, and neither money, influence, fame, nor time can erase the deeds of two decades ago or two years ago. Today is a new day. You can start over. But save yourself much heartache by making careful and prayerful decisions each day.

Unfortunately, the only way to learn to select the right choice is by doing it—over and over again. Fortunately, there is help available: "Jesus said . . . 'I am the way, the truth, and the life. No one comes to the Father except through Me' " (John 14:6).

The Way . . .

Jesus provides the *direction* you are looking for in your life. You must "choose for [yourself] this day whom you will serve" (Josh. 24:15). Peer pressure plays an enormous role in decision-making. Many people buy clothes that they think others will like; wear their hair in the newest style of the group; talk, walk, and act like their friends. This is not bad, to a point.

Never let a "friend" influence you against the direction God has for you, which is to serve Him. You must make the decision to say "no" on a date to sex, drugs, or wild parties *before* you even accept the date. If you wait until you are confronted with the situation, it may be too late.

In the *Phantom of the Opera*, actor Michael Crawford seductively sings, "The Point of No Return," which talks about the power of temptation and its ability to trap us. Waiting until temptation confronts you to make a moral decision is flirting with the point of no return.

The Truth . . .

Jesus helps in the *decisions* of life. He said to "let your 'Yes' be 'Yes,' and your 'No,' 'No.' For whatever is more than these is from the evil one" (Matt. 5:37). Procrastinating, vacillating from one answer to another, and trying to please everyone will only cause problems and cannot be the wisdom of God. James 1:5, 8 instructs us to ask God for wisdom and He will liberally give it, but to be "double-minded" is to be unstable in every area of life. Choose now to do God's will as He reveals it to you with no adjustments or waiting on your part.

The Life . . .

Jesus wants to eliminate the *dullness* of life. I meet teens every week who are afraid that living for Jesus will be boring. They have mental pictures of sitting in their rooms, staring at blank walls, and stifling their creative urges. Nothing could be further from the life God has planned for you. His desire is for you to *aim high* in all aspects of life. He wants to do away with the dullness of life.

Society is trying to program you to believe that to enjoy life you must be breathtakingly beautiful (or handsome), have a fabulous home and car, and buy your clothes from all the "right" designers. But you can qualify on each point and be very *unhappy*, or qualify on each point and be very *happy*. How can both be true?

"If anyone loves the world, the love of the Father is not in him" (1 John 2:15). It's okay to "like" the things money can buy, but being addicted to materialism is another thing completely. Too many people seem to have lost the "wonder" of life as seen through the eyes of a child. Instead they have to manufacture and buy happiness.

The love of the world can literally choke the joy from life. So many individuals are struggling because they are more concerned about what the world thinks than about God's standard for living.

Joy in life is available to you right now, regardless of your circumstances. It is not a where, when, or how much. Carry that idea further to see that happiness often depends on circumstances, but true joy in life transcends all situations, good or bad. The source of joy is found in God, for He never changes.

Isn't it good to know that when all around you changes—friends, job situations, the "right look," the economy—*God never changes*. Jesus said, "I have come that they may have life, and that they may have it more abundantly" (John 10:10). God's love and desire for you to *aim high* are constant.

Come to the Father . . .

Jesus reminds us of the *dimensions* of life. As we become so absorbed in what this life has to offer, we lose sight of the fact that we were created to spend eternity with God. We really are just passing through here.

And so, while we strive to be the best to the glory of God, we remember that our motives must always have eternity and pleasing Him as their focus.

This period should be the greatest of your life. You are rapidly approaching the end of the bridge between childhood and adulthood. Making right choices keeps you from jumping off.

Sometimes we feel "dizzy" from all of the options we have to consider. To quote *Megatrends* author John Naisbitt, "In today's 'Baskin-Robbins' society,' everything comes in at least 31 flavors." He explains that until the

1960s people had few decisions to make; it was an either/or world:

- Either we got married or we did not.
- Either we worked nine to five on a regular job or we just didn't work.
- Ford or Chevy.
- Chocolate or vanilla.

But now the world of multiple options confronts us.

When the "dizziness" starts, clear your mind and go back to the basics. Too many decisions about too many unimportant choices will confuse you and keep you from *aiming high*. There are four basic choices that every person will have to make:

1. What will I do with my life vocationally?
2. How much education will I pursue?
3. Will I marry, and if so, whom will I marry?
4. What principles and guidelines will I live by?

Don't let the quickening pace of this generation deceive you into believing that your life or the events of the world are beyond your control. Change causes you to think, to evaluate, to choose. By learning to make proper choices, you harness change and use it to your benefit.

5

FINDING GOD'S WILL

A rapidly changing world can be confusing. Sometimes it seems that everything that has been nailed down is coming loose. Especially when those you respect, believe in, and look up to suddenly disappoint you through their behavior, you may have a difficult time understanding what's going on. You may feel betrayed and hurt. When tragedy strikes someone you know, you may question God. When problems come that you can't seem to deal with or solve, you may wonder if He really cares for you. You may even attribute sin and imperfection to the holy, perfect God.

However confused or disappointed you may feel, you can rest in the fact that God loves you with an "everlasting love" and has a plan for you. According to Psalm 139, He knew you while you were still in the womb, and His thoughts of you are precious and great.

As you accept the fact that God loves you and has a plan for you personally, a design for you individually that He urgently wants you to discover, you will have less of a job trying to find it.

Whatever God's will for your life is, you can be sure that it is *perfect* for you *right now*. He wants to answer your questions about marriage, career, and goals. The explanations are not so difficult once you know the formula:

P ray in faith.

E xamine the Scriptures.

R eceive Christ.

F ill your life with the Spirit.

E valuate the circumstances.

C onfess sin.

T alk to godly counsel.

Pray in Faith.

If you really want God's best for yourself, you will urgently pray each day until the answer is clear. Praying urgently is not the same as begging and crying. It is sincere, from the heart, talking with God. Many times as you pray, God allows you to see your true feelings about the subject so you see that the thing you so desperately wanted is not right at all for the time.

James 1:5 indicates you are to ask in faith in order to receive the wisdom of God from above. Proverbs 3:5,6 states,

> Trust in the LORD with all your heart,
> And lean not on your own understanding;
> In all your ways acknowledge Him,
> And He shall direct your paths.

Prayer is total abandon to the will of God as you ask clear

direction. It is an open heart telling God the need and listening closely for the answer. Faith is believing that the sovereign God is in control of this world and of your life. Ask yourself, Just how much quality time do I spend in prayer asking God to reveal His will?

Examine the Scriptures.

"Be diligent to present yourself approved to God, a worker who does not need to be ashamed, rightly dividing the word of truth" (2 Tim. 2:15). Knowing the Word of God keeps you from being ashamed because it keeps you from getting into circumstances that God has already condemned. So many Christians are embarrassed and ashamed because they have been caught in sin.

God intends for every Christian to be a student of the Bible. To "rightly divide" is a jeweler's term, which means "to work with precision." That means an occasional look at Scripture or a casual reading of devotionals won't cut it. You need to study the Bible regularly. And when you do, it will help keep you from sin. Remember, it's sin that keeps you from the Word of God.

What does the Bible have to say about dating, finances, marriage, and friendships? You can become confused and unsure because you don't carefully study the teachings already provided.

The first test of whether or not a situation is in the will of God is to ask yourself if it is consistent with the Word of God. Is it Christ-honoring? So many times individuals struggle with decisions already clearly decided and stated by God. The first place to turn in seeking God's will is to the Bible itself.

Receive Christ.

If you have tried to pray and have tried to read your Bible without success, perhaps you have never actually come to know Christ on a one-to-one, personal basis. Perhaps you have not received Christ as your Savior.

God's will for all is to come to Him in salvation, to experience forgiveness and healing, to find purpose and life, to escape hell and be offered heaven. But God has given human beings the power to have a free will. We are not puppets; we have the choice of accepting His gift of grace through the Cross or rejecting it.

Fill Your Life with the Spirit.

You are also charged to be filled with the Spirit of God. If this sounds like something you do at a gas station, you're on the right track! When a vessel is filled, it is saturated with a substance so that no other matter can be added.

To be filled with God's Spirit is to allow Him to fill your thought life, dating life, habits, and total being. When you are filled with the Spirit, you are sensitive to God's leading.

Jesus promised to send a comforter, a teacher, who would "guide you into all truth" (John 16:13). How will He guide? Through prayer, the Scriptures, circumstances, and counsel.

Evaluate the Circumstances.

Scrutinize the circumstances you are asking God to direct you in. Examine them carefully to see if, first of all, they are compatible with the Word of God. Too often you may struggle with decisions already clearly decided and stated by God. These are not negotiable. No matter how many ways you twist it for your own use, God's Word stands strong and immovable. It is given for instruction and correction in the standard of God, not the standard of what you want.

Immorality is clearly defined as sin in the Bible, but there are many aspects of life for which there are no specific biblical instructions, such as career choices, education, and the timing of your decisions. You must determine these by a combination of events.

Falling in love, or thinking you're in love, can be the most dangerous ruler you will ever use in determining God's plan. Ideas like, "It can't be wrong if it feels so good," are based on man's "If it feels good, do it" attitude. The writer of Proverbs rightly observed, "There is a way which seems right to a man, / But its end is the way of death" (Prov. 14:12).

In fact, many of the problems you now face are the results of your own actions. One of the most difficult things in life is to accept the blame for the mess you are in. It is easier to blame God for not keeping you out of it, accuse friends of bad advice, and so on. But the good news is that God will help you find a way out if you allow Him by yielding yourself to Him.

Above all, remember that God has infallibly promised to order "for good" the lives of those who truly love Him (Prov. 3:5,6; Rom. 8:28).

Confess Sin.

When the Holy Spirit moves in your heart, the first thing He does is to convict you of your sin. Sin blocks fellowship with God and, therefore, keeps you from knowing His perfect will for your life. You cannot assume that God will reveal anything to you until you have recognized His first promptings, that is, to cleanse your heart of sin.

Secular society has tried to eliminate the word *sin* from our vocabulary. The New Age Movement teaches that people are good and not sinners. But Romans 3:23 teaches that "all have sinned and fall short of the glory of God."

Sin is as much an attitude as an action. Sin can be acts of omission (things you should do, but don't) as well as commission (things you should not do, but do). The Bible defines *sin* literally as to "miss the mark." It is the picture of an expert marksman aiming with all his concentration but failing to hit his target. *Sin keeps you from aiming high.*

Sin is like leprosy or cancer; it begins with small blemishes or small groups of abnormal cells, then begins to destroy the body. Daily ask God to cleanse your heart of sin, small or not, so that the line of communication can be clear.

Talk to Godly Counsel.

You may seek advice about a decision only because you hope, by asking many times, you will eventually receive the answer you desire. Seeking advice is an excellent help in determining God's will, but seek godly counsel. Talk to your pastor, youth worker, Sunday school teacher, or other leaders in your school or church. God has given parents for this very reason (believe it or not), so that He might speak to you through their authority and experience.

Friends with their advice can be comforting, but they can also be wrong. Use the same test on the advice of others as you do on your own feelings as you seek to know God's *perfect* will for you.

There are three common denominators for every Christian:

1. *Morals.* God's will is for you to be morally pure.
2. *Ministry.* As you present yourself to Him, remember that God has a definite plan of service for each of His children.
3. *Might.* Live in the might of the Spirit, the power that God made available to you through salvation.

Although the Word of God is the final word on decisions of life, in areas where there is no specific revelation, you must depend on prayer, circumstances, *and* godly counsel. One of the three is not enough.

It is equally important to trust God for your decision, regardless of what the outcome may be. Jesus prayed, "Father . . . not My will, but Yours, be done" (Luke 22:42). You can accomplish this only when you realize how very much God loves you and wants the best for your life. Faith and obedience go together, and in His time and in His way His will becomes plain.

6

TODAY IS THE DAY

This generation sings, "Tonight's the night"—the night to party, to have sex, to use and abuse drugs. The Creator tells us, "Today is the day"—the day of living right.

It is a day of awesome responsibility and electrifying opportunities. Former Secretary of State Dean Rusk once challenged a group of high school students interested in government with these words:

> I would like to suggest to the young people here this evening that more is going to be asked of you than from any other generation in history because the entire human race is now facing a series of problems which are different in kind from any the human race has faced before.

Problems Equal Opportunities.

In the quest to find a cure for cancer, tremendous discoveries have been made which are useful in many other problem-solving situations. In fact, every weakness of the human race—whether it has been related to health, finances, the environment, peace, technology, or whatever—has spurred us on to new heights in innovation.

The future stretches before us in a sea of vast and

countless opportunities, waiting for us to investigate and expand in knowledge.

Our word *opportunity* is from the Latin word *opportunus*, meaning "favorable." The picture is of favorable winds blowing a ship in the correct direction. But we have seen evidence that an opportunity may result from unfavorable winds. Only the closing of our eyes, the lethargy of our minds, the dulling of our spirits, can stop us.

Now more than ever we need young men and young women who are determined to make a difference. *Will you have an effect on the changes in the world, or will you be affected by the changes?* We are in desperate need of strong, determined, morally pure, hard-working leaders.

Harvard president Derek Bok stated, "There is a very obvious dearth of people who seem to be able to supply convincing answers or even point in the direction of solutions." There is an endangered species in the world that we have yet to protect or put on any list: quality leaders.

The concern for leaders was apparent in the days of Joshua. The time of transition in leadership was one of the most critical periods in the history of Israel. The children of Israel stood in shock and uncertainty at the death of Moses, their leader for forty years.

As the people mourned in fear of the future, the young man Joshua stood tall and accepted the challenge to *aim high.* The historical record shows that Joshua picked up where Moses left off.

He led the people of Israel from the wilderness, across the Jordan, and into the Promised Land, and his capabilities and daring took them through three major military campaigns involving more than thirty enemy armies. Before the journey began, he warned them that there would be many battles ahead before entering the Promised Land, and he said, "Sanctify yourselves, for tomorrow the LORD will do wonders among you" (Josh. 3:5).

That verse was true then, and it is equally appropriate today. If you want the blessings of God on your tomorrow, *set yourself apart for God's service today.*

How do you do that? Sit in a room and wait for a vision or a revelation? Never! Instead, your total being will be involved:

Program your mind.

Present your body.

Prove what you are made of.

What Paul said to the Roman Christians centuries ago still applies today:

> I beseech you therefore, brethren, by the mercies of God, that you present your bodies a living sacrifice, holy, acceptable to God, which is your reasonable service. And do not be conformed to this world, but be transformed by the renewing of your mind, that you may prove what is that good and acceptable and perfect will of God (Rom. 12:1,2).

Program Your Mind.

"Be transformed by the renewing of your mind." You have already seen how important it is for you to control your thoughts and how your attitude determines your motivation. This is another area that influences your actions.

Dr. Nelson Price, pastor of the Roswell Street Baptist Church in Atlanta, has observed, "Inventor Thomas Edison once said, 'The chief purpose of the body is to carry the brain around.' If this is true, then never has so much attention been given to the vehicle and so little to the cargo. Our society has a poor sense of priorities. We parade our bodies; we fussily dress them, exercise them, nourish them, and protect them with medicines. With all the pomp and circumstance given to the body, we seem to have forgotten that without the brain, the body ceases to function."

Little attention is given to the fountain of life—the brain. Yet scientists have discovered that each person was created with the capacity to store *all* known information.

The storing of wrong information is one reason why the brain is not used to its capacity. The morals fed into the brain can and will affect the ability to lead. The guilt and shame associated with sin can cause you to fail in your quest for the best *unless you prepare ahead of time.* There are many temptations that will affect your mind, and you must lay up ammunition to say "no" in the world's battle for your mind.

One of the easiest mind battles to lose is the use of mind- and mood-altering drugs. This includes the use of alcoholic beverages because alcohol itself is a drug, one of the deadliest. Most people turn on for basically the same reasons:

P ressure

E scape

A vailability

C uriosity

E mptiness

Pressure

The pressure to drink and use drugs is great. It seems as if from every side you are urged to "follow the crowd." Advertisements, movies, television, and today's music portray drinking as glamorous and exciting.

In addition to outside pressures, there are pressures from within. Restlessness, boredom, reactions to home restrictions, and the desire to try something new are strong in most young people. Whatever the reasons, alcohol and drug abuse by youths and adults is one of the biggest problems facing the Western world.

Escape

These are the years of new responsibility. You are beginning to solve your own problems. Change is occurring rapidly. Many young people do not feel adequate to cope with these demands and are not willing or able to accept these new duties; so, they "run away" through drug use.

Availability

Drugs are accessible at schools, most parties, virtually every hangout. In some states, alcohol is legal for the older graduate, but does that mean you should drink it? *Just because some of your friends have given in doesn't mean you should.*

Curiosity

Many young people try drugs and alcohol just for a new experience. "If everyone else does it, I want to try it, too!" is a too-common refrain.

Emptiness

The first four reasons give insight as to why many begin using mind-altering chemicals, but emptiness is the reason many continue. They stay on drugs because they see no reason not to or because they see no other solution to their problems. They exist in a psychological and spiritual desert. This aimless desperation has caused millions to hide behind a chemical curtain or drown in a sea of alcohol.

Radio, TV, magazines, and peers have tried the soft sell. The beer commercials are really the funniest advertising on television; the wine commercials are among the sexiest. All are sprayed with a "glitter," never exposing the dirty side of alcohol and drug use.

Don't be fooled. A great percentage of those in prison are there for crimes committed while under the influence. Many cannot even remember the crime or the events preceding it. And many unwanted pregnancies began on a night of "partying."

Using alcohol looks so fun, so cool, so great. You believe you can control it, but soon it controls you. Paul warned, "And do not be drunk with wine, in which is dissipation; but be filled with the Spirit" (Eph. 5:18).

Guard your mind so that nothing will distract you from your goal of being the best you can be. We all need peace from the stresses of the world. But don't be deceived. The false peace that comes from drugs is only momentary at best; the peace that Jesus gives is secure and lasting.

Present Your Body.

In the same way the media sell alcohol, they sell premarital sex. Sometimes it occurs very subtly in commercials: the girl calls to let her boyfriend know that no one is at home and he rushes over, or the young girl wears very tight jeans that provoke lusty stares. Often it's very blatant—in sitcoms where all the petting is shown or in movies where nothing is left to the imagination.

The temptation is placed before you daily. Today is the day to make the decision about your moral life.

The temptation is so great because everyone is affected by what is seen and heard. *You must become more selective in what you allow to occupy your mind and, therefore, determine your morality.* Immoral thoughts may come to mind, but you have the power to stop them right there. End the desire before it becomes sin.

It is important to learn to control yourself. An uncontrolled person may bring great harm to himself or herself and others. Sexual thoughts and desires are no different from other thoughts in terms of needing control. Food appetites must be controlled, or you endanger your physical health. Spending habits must be controlled, or you will be financially bankrupt. Thoughts must be controlled, or you may become emotionally unbalanced. Actions must be controlled to avoid spiritual suicide. The need for control of sexual thoughts and desires does not end at marriage because many circumstances, such as pregnancy, illness, children, traveling, and work schedules, will make it necessary.

Possibly the best way to overcome wrong thoughts and desires is to avoid temptation as much as possible. Stay away from acquaintances who encourage you wrongly; don't put yourself in compromising situations with the person to whom you are sexually attracted; throw away tempting magazines and books. In short, avoid situations that might cause you to fall: "Flee also youthful lusts; but pursue righteousness, faith, love, peace with those who call on the Lord out of a pure heart" (2 Tim. 2:22).

The only way to totally rid your mind of evil thoughts is to reprogram your mind with good thoughts, the Bible. The Word of God is alive and powerful and can direct your heart (Heb. 4:12). It gives us strength to overcome sin (Eph. 6:17; Ps. 119:11). It offers hope and direction during times of struggle (Rom. 15:4). As a result of studying and obeying the Word of God, we will achieve God's goals for our lives, according to God's promise (Josh. 1:8).

There are many ways to study the Word of God, but without consistency, none of them will suffice: hear the Word taught, read the Scriptures, memorize verses. Any time you learn the Word of God, take the time to *apply* the passages: how do these words affect my world, my church, or my Christian life in general and in particular? As a result of reading these passages, what action must I take to comply with what they say? If you are serious about aiming high, commit to working hard at overcoming temptation.

First, there is the very real risk of pregnancy. Don't be foolish enough to think it can't happen to you. It can, on the first time, on the fifth time, anytime. It is possible.

Second, the sin of premarital sex cheapens your testimony. There will definitely be talk about your actions, no matter how discreet you think you may be. Is this the way you want to represent Christ in your life?

Third, once you give in to a sexual relationship outside marriage, you make it easier for yourself to fall into the sin again and again. Saying "no" the first time is difficult, but once you have ignored your conscience, it will be increasingly easier to continue. You are introducing yourself to a lifestyle that you were never meant to experience as a Christian. *You begin a life of rebellion against God.*

Finally, as soon as you begin a sexual relationship, you diminish the strengthening of the other areas of your relationship. Knowing each other intimately involves so much more than sex. What are the goals in your lives? What habits do you have that might be annoying to the other? Are the ideals and ethics of your lives the same? Do you have the same thoughts on raising children?

There are so many avenues to explore in the dating relationship as you prepare for marriage. Many divorces are the result of incompatibility—aspects about each other learned after marriage that were not explored in dating because the two were drawn together by a sexual relationship. Such a relationship offers a counterfeit completeness, a false closeness that is often mistaken for love. Sexual pleasure can be strong enough to mask and overshadow basic and conflicting differences in your personalities.

One fact that most young people overlook: no one has a guarantee of tomorrow. At the close of a crusade in Alabama, two beautiful young ladies approached the podium to talk with me.

The first one told me her story. Planning to marry within the year, she and her boyfriend began a sexual relationship. He bought her a ring; she picked out the dress; everything was set. Only one problem—she became pregnant and he decided he wasn't ready for all the responsibility. Her dreams were shattered and her future sharply altered.

The second young lady listened in tears. Her story was similar. She and her fiancé had been dating for three years, and now that the wedding was set, they saw no reason to wait any longer to have sex. Then suddenly, tragically, he was killed in an accident. She had to pick up the pieces and start over, but the memories of stolen sex continued to haunt her.

Perhaps you have no intention of "going all the way," but you do like to flirt with the idea and enjoy the petting. Just how far is "too far" on a date? Again, the standard is God's Word: "Flee sexual immorality" (1 Cor. 6:18).

First of all, consider the character of the person you are dating. You have put your stamp of approval on the individual by accepting the date. But do you really know what values he or she lives by? A large percentage of rapes are committed, not by strangers, but by males who already know their victims. A "really nice guy" can be changed drastically by drug use or alcohol. Don't be naive enough to think it can't happen to you; statistics prove no one is exempt from the possibility.

Be wary of attraction to those who are in trouble. The parental instinct causes these feelings. You may feel that you can help or that you are "needed." As a Christian, you can help, but as a date, you are in danger of being used or even seduced.

Don't tempt yourself by getting involved in potentially compromising situations. For example, never be alone at home with a date. Many good intentions have been forgotten because the temptation and opportunity were too great. The same applies to parking and petting. Sexual feelings are being stirred up that cannot morally be fulfilled.

Petting with everyone you are attracted to will soon lead to an abused mind, body, and personality. You cannot allow your person to be used by others.

James pretty well summed it up: "But each one is tempted when he is drawn away by his own desires and enticed. Then, when desire has conceived, it gives birth to sin; and sin, when it is full-grown, brings forth death. Do not be deceived, my beloved brethren" (James 1:14–16). Don't give sin a chance to become full-grown and dangerous.

Prove What You Are Made Of.

There must be a time in every life when the boy or girl steps out of the picture and the man or woman takes over. It is the "metamorphosis," if you will, of life.

Once and for all, decide to live a pure life, a life set apart for God, and never waiver from that standard. Before you strive for that standard, though, make sure that you have made the most important decision of all time: give yourself to Christ and receive Him as your personal Savior.

Jesus Himself called it being "born again" (John 3:3). He instructed Nicodemus, a very moral man, to be born again before attempting to live for God. Jesus lovingly took the time to explain that just as we are born into a physical family, we must be born again into a spiritual family, God's family of believers.

The Bible says that "all have sinned." There is no exception. Christ died for that sin, and by faith, each of us may receive the gift of salvation.

Jesus Himself extends the invitation to you: "Behold, I stand at the door and knock. If anyone hears My voice and opens the door, I will come in to him and dine with him, and he with Me" (Rev. 3:20). The door is the door of your heart, and the dining signifies fellowship and a relationship. Here is a sample prayer you can pray to receive Christ, or you can pray in your own words. Jesus is more concerned with the faith of your heart than with what you say with your mouth.

> Dear Lord, thank You for loving me. Thank You for dying on the cross for me. I know I am a sinner and cannot save myself. Please forgive all my sin. Please come into my heart, save me, and change me. I give my life to You, to follow You for the rest of my life. Help me to live for You and to tell others what You have done for me this moment. Thank You for answering my prayer and saving me, for I pray it in Jesus' name. Amen.

You can be sure of your salvation because it was promised by God: "For 'whoever calls upon the name of the LORD shall be saved' " (Rom. 10:13).

After receiving this new life in Christ, you are admonished, "Don't let the world squeeze you into its own mold, but let God re-make you so that . . . your mind is changed" (Rom. 12:2, PHILLIPS). Begin now to live, not only for this age, but for the age to come—eternity.

As you *aim high*, stand by your beliefs and urge others to join you instead of your joining them. As you build toward the future, take care of what you have constructed on a daily basis so that once you reach the top, your foundation will remain strong.

Dr. Joel Gregory, a great scholar and preacher, has shared a great example of this principle:

> One of the old and magnificent ruined castles of Ireland came to a strange end. It was the ancient home of the Castlereagh family, one of the most princely residences on the Emerald Isle. But the ancient home fell into decay and was no longer inhabited.
>
> The usual happened. When the peasants wanted to repair a road, build a chimney, or pig-sty, they would scavenge stones from the fine old castle. The stones were already

craftily cut, finished and fit. Best of all, they were available without digging and carrying for miles.

One day Lord Londonderry visited his castle. He was the surviving descendant and heir. When he saw the state of his ancestral home, he determined to end immediately the robbery of the building for its stones. The ruin itself reflected the earlier glories of his family and was one of the treasures of Ireland. He sent for his agent and gave orders for the castle to be enclosed with a wall six feet tall and well coped. This would keep out the trespassers. He went on his way.

Three or four years later he returned. To his astonishment the castle was gone, completely disappeared, vanished into the air. In its place there was a huge wall enclosing nothing. He sent for his agent and demanded to know why his orders had not been carried out. The agent insisted they had been. "But where is the castle?" asked the Lord. "The castle, is it? I built the wall with it, my Lord! Is it for me to be going miles for materials with the finest stones in Ireland beside me?"

Lord Londonderry had his wall—but the castle, without which the wall meant nothing, had disappeared.

If you achieve your goals but set aside the principles of God to get there, you have destroyed your castle and are left with only a wall.

Today is the day to stand tall that all the world might see the glory of God *in you*!

7

QUEST FOR THE RAINBOW

Irish legend has it that at the end of every rainbow is a pot of gold, hidden there by a tiny leprechaun. The Land of Oz was a magical land "somewhere over the rainbow." Throughout the ages, poets and philosophers have been fascinated by the majesty and mystery of the rainbow. Only a handful have ever been able to adequately describe its beauty and magic.

This book has challenged you to dream, to begin your quest for the best in life. This chapter reveals the formula for finding the elusive happiness and wealth at the rainbow's end.

In the world-famous motivational classic *Acres of Diamonds*, author Russell H. Conwell shares the secret of the search for happiness. The story is told of an American youth traveling down the Tigris and Euphrates rivers guided by an Arab of Baghdad. The aged guide was talkative and took delight in telling one story after another. One was of particular interest to Conwell.

Ali Hafed was a successful Persian farmer. He had heard of the immense wealth that the possession of diamonds could bring, and he became fascinated with the idea. Having been told that with one diamond the size of a thumb you could purchase the whole country, he imagined that with a mine of diamonds the world could be his for the asking.

Ali Hafed went to bed that night a poor man. He still had his farm, but he was poor because of his discontent with what he had. He became obsessed with the vision of vast wealth diamonds could bring to him. No longer content to earn a living with his farm, flocks, orchards, and fields, he sold the farm. He left behind family and friends and began a journey that took him around the world in search of diamonds and great wealth.

At the end of a fruitless and long journey, Hafed was bankrupt, wretched, and starving. Having given up family, friends, and a profitable business, he cast himself into the sea of foam and salt never to rise in this life again.

What a depressing story! But wait . . . there is more.

The purchaser of Hafed's farm set to work plowing and planting. One day, while working, he discovered a black stone. Holding it up for closer inspection, he noticed that it reflected all the hues of the rainbow. Thinking it quite pretty, he cleaned it and placed it on his mantel as an ornament.

Days later, a priest (coincidentally the same one who started Hafed on his journey) was visiting the farmer's home. Noticing the stone on the mantel, he inspected it more closely and then began to shout. "Has Hafed returned and discovered diamonds?" he quickly asked. "No," the farmer explained, "I found that stone in the back yard."

As they searched the back yard, they discovered hundreds of diamonds. That farm became the most magnificent diamond mine in all of the world. In fact, the crown jewels of Russia and England were found there.

Imagine, if Ali Hafed had worked his own resources

instead of embarking on a fruitless search for "instant wealth," he would have discovered acres of diamonds rather than frustration and misery.

Rarely does a get-rich-quick scheme ever produce. There are few shortcuts to be found on the road to achievement. Many graduates will gamble all they have looking for that one-in-a-million "deal" that will bring the pot of gold at the end of the rainbow.

Happiness can indeed be found in one's own back yard without sacrificing an ounce of potential. It is much simpler to pack up and "get out of here" in search of new horizons, all the while grumbling, "My parents don't understand" or "Nothing ever happens here."

If you can't be happy here and now, you won't be happy there and then. Even the rainbow can attest to that. It is not well known, but it is a scientific fact that the rainbow is actually a complete circle, reaching farther than the eye can see. Just as the rainbow circles around, the graduate can see that the beginning is in your own back yard—with the resources, the family, and the friends you have already been given.

If that sounds boring to you, read on. It is also a scientific fact that two people, standing side by side admiring the same rainbow, are actually seeing light refracted and reflected by different sets of raindrops. *Each individual has a personal rainbow.*

In the same way, each person has unique experiences, sorrows, and talents and abilities that mold and shape the future. God wants you to "bloom where you are planted." He wants you—right where you are—to be all that you can be for Him. Only when you have made full use of the talents and opportunities He has already given you will you receive more.

Jesus made this clear when He told the parable of the talents (in this case, money) in Matthew 25. A man left his servants in charge of his goods as he traveled abroad. To one servant, he gave five talents; to another, two; and to another, one.

Upon returning he found the first servant had doubled his investment, and so had the second one. He congratulated and promoted each of them.

The third servant, however, had hidden his talent in the ground for safekeeping. He had not used his resource at all and, consequently, had nothing to show for it. The master took the talent away from the servant and gave it to another.

Whatever your talents, they are uniquely and distinctively yours. Discover them; cultivate them to the fullest. In the quest for the rainbow, you may learn of the talents of others, but be what *you* can be.

Develop what you are good at and what you enjoy.

Use your gifts. Be grateful for family and friends. Exhaust your talents and expect God to give you more.

As you search for new opportunities and develop new talents, look particularly for significance in all that you do. The quest for significance is the quest to be the best at what you do and how you do it.

Sears often advertises three levels of quality for the same product: "good, better, and best." *Why settle for "good" or "better" when you can have "best"?*

Significance is not equal to recognition. When the motive is for recognition, the heart begins to exist on pride and prejudice. To be the best you can be, you will want others to succeed as well. To motivate yourself, encourage others. As you inspire them, you will be inspired.

A people-helper finds joy and purpose in assisting

those around her. A balcony person will build up and be lifted up. A basement person tears others down and abases himself.

Three truths can transform your attitude about your station in life at this moment:

1. *God can do it.* He is sovereign. God knows what He's doing and He is doing it. By faith, I trust in His care.
2. *God can do it through me.* He has made me in His image, created for good works. I am equally important to His plan as anyone else.
3. *God can do it through me now, right where I am.* I can begin now with the talents, resources, and relationships I have, knowing that God will supply an increase as I am faithful to Him.

The prize is not a rainbow in the sky, but the "upward call of God in Christ Jesus" (Phil. 3:14). You are not to chase the legends and stories of the world, but to put your hope and labor into your own rainbows. The race for the world's gold leads only to an empty pot. God offers you peace in the knowledge that where He places you is where He wants you to begin to grow.

8

THE SPIRIT OF NEVERTHELESS

Aim high; aim to win! But when along the way you encounter roadblocks and detours, you must continue in the spirit of David.

David was described as a man with a concept that captivated his mind, a principle that compelled him, a mission of accomplishment. David was known to have "the spirit of nevertheless."

This spirit explains the success in his life. David became one of the greatest leaders in history. This spirit led him from a mere lad to a leader, from the pasture to the palace, from a shepherd to a sovereign. This very ordinary guy from an ordinary family accomplished the extraordinary.

Whether or not you declare the spirit of nevertheless as your own will determine how you will handle your future challenges and opportunities. Consider David.

David was often underestimated by advisers and adversaries. He was an able military leader, political leader, and king, and best of all, he was "a man after [God's] own heart" (1 Sam. 13:14). Yet he was defied by foes and discouraged by friends.

David's every undertaking was met with criticism. His vision was so great, few could join him in it. David chose to stick with his plan in spite of constant urging otherwise.

When Saul was plotting to kill David, David's followers urged him to slay Saul first. He had more than one opportunity to do so, but believed in his heart that God had another plan. David was, of course, right, and God rewarded him for enduring in the spirit of nevertheless.

Are you bombarded with "free advice"? Don't let anyone, I repeat, *anyone*, distract you from the path God has set before you.

There are four basic types of people who will surround you in your quest for the best:

1. *The failers*
2. *The figurers*
3. *The feelers*
4. *The faithers*

1. *The failers* might even include persons close to you—those who never quite make their goal, those who always have an excuse as to why they failed. Don't listen to their chorus of discouragement or allow it to dampen your enthusiasm.

Have you ever watched a sporting event where a player fumbled the ball or made a very obvious mistake? To cover it up, the player will sometimes use the "loser's limp." All of a sudden, there is an announcement of a leg injury, and he is assisted in walking off the field. His recovery is usually quick, and he is back playing again, but the injury is blamed for the error.

The failers may attempt great things, but give up at the first difficulty. Because they are discouraged, they will try to discourage you. Don't be surprised if this group is not excited about your dreams or accomplishments.

2. *The figurers* are individuals who have it all written in

black and white. "It won't work," they say, "according to my figures. My calculations show this to be impossible."

The figurers advised David, "The fortress is too strong. The hill is too high. We will lose too many men. It's not worth the risk." Stay away from these kind of friends.

The Mary Kay Cosmetics Company in Dallas is famous around the world for its beauty products. It is also well known for giving pink Cadillacs and furs to the highest achievers of sales each year. Mary Kay Ash began her company with a dream and a vision and very little else. As she set up her company, her accountant told her she would be out of business in a month. "Your plan won't work. You're giving away too much money." And my favorite one: "It's never been done that way before." Recently the company celebrated its 25th anniversary and is now a multi-million-dollar business. Obviously, the accountant was wrong.

3. *The feelers* told David, "This sounds like a good idea, but we just don't *feel good* about it. This isn't a good time. We just had a civil war, you know."

The feelers also let how they feel affect their personal lives. Their emotions are tossed about as quickly as a change in the wind. Every circumstance in life affects their mood. As a result, they are either elated or depressed— seldom in between. They feel like either a million dollars or small change.

Feelings are too unreliable to use in accurately evaluating an endeavor or an action.

4. *The faithers* are few. David was a forerunner in this group. He believed in the Lord and in himself: "Nevertheless David took the stronghold" (2 Sam. 5:7). In his battles against King Saul, Jebusites, Goliath, and multiple enemies, David never contemplated defeat.

This group is made up of leaders, but unfortunately, it has the fewest members. Nevertheless, they seem to rely on this advice:

> Stand therefore, having girded your waist with truth, having put on the breastplate of righteousness, and having shod your feet with the preparation of the gospel of peace; above all, taking the shield of faith with which you will be able to quench all the fiery darts of the wicked one (Eph. 6:14-16).

Regardless of your situation, you must move ahead and capture your goals. You must go forward, guided by the will of God, strengthened by faith.

9

SHAKE OFF THE DUST

Shake off the dust,
Leave your troubles far behind,
Shake off the dust,
You can do it if you try.
Shake off the dust,
And let your spirit fly!
                    —*"Shake Off The Dust"*
                    Sung by Truth

As you pack your belongings for college, a new apartment, or the military, there is one box better left behind. It is the box that contains the pain of your past.

Most of the people I meet are struggling to shake off the dust from their lives and don't seem able to escape their problems. Some can't even talk about them. Others can talk, but seem incapable of doing anything about their problems.

There is a story in the Bible about a woman who was bent over for many years (Luke 13:10–13). She spent all her time looking down at the dirt; that is, until Jesus one day healed her and straightened her up. Most people are like that woman. They can see only themselves and their problems. They don't look up and see how close their salvation really is.

As a teenage junkie, I finally looked up and saw Jesus Christ. I want to help you see that there is hope for a better life. You don't have to remain victimized by your past. Whatever has gone wrong can be made right. Some problems involve the scars of memory. They are the results of things done to you by others. And some are the consequences of things you have done to yourself. Each problem is unique, but all can be solved in Christ. *You can make peace with your past and get on with the rest of your life.*

There are two types of wounds that will be fatal if left untreated.

First, there are experiences in the past in which individuals were wounded by the actions of others. These are the hurts in which they were the *victims*. Many people have to struggle with painful memories of an ugly divorce, separations, and rejection. Others have been abused physically, emotionally, and sexually.

I personally have been through all of these and can relate to the hurt you feel. It is natural for you to be affected by these hurts. You may have been beaten down emotionally and now struggle with a poor self-image. Being told all your life that you won't amount to anything does not have to be a self-fulfilling prophecy, however.

The tragedy of such a past is that the story doesn't end here. Often because of the hurt, people attempt to drown the problems to dull the pain, to "party away" the powerful effects of the wounds.

It is not uncommon for a young boy who has been sexually abused to have a confused sexual identity and turn to homosexuality. A young girl who has been molested, particularly in an incestuous situation, may turn to prostitution or allow herself to be passed around like a pack of cigarettes in order to feel love because she feels that is all she is worthy of. Or she may feel unable to ever have a meaningful relationship.

Statistics overwhelmingly support the fact that young people who have been raised in an alcoholic environment often turn to drugs and alcohol themselves. Those who have been abused often end up abusing their own children or someone else's. Children of divorced parents are more susceptible to divorce when they reach adulthood.

The second type of wound occurs when those who have been victims frequently become the *villains* by hurting themselves. They injure themselves and rob themselves of any peace in the future. They become the Jesse James of their own lives. The Bible calls this sin.

Others don't even have the convenience of an alibi. In their quest for pleasure and acceptance, a lifestyle of pain and disrepute has resulted. Every week I meet college students who have turned their backs on the truth and standards of their upbringing to become part of the cult of self-fulfillment. They have been blinded by the glitter of the "scene."

After leaving the rules of their parents, many adopt the thinking of Adam and Eve—"I'm missing out on the good times." Just as Adam and Eve ate of the forbidden fruit, so they investigate forbidden pleasures on their own. And they must eventually deal with heartache and shame.

Even if you have rejected God's way and will for your life in the past, there is good news for the present. The essence of the Bible is that *no matter who you are, what you have done or gone through, or what kind of mess you are in, you can be cleansed, forgiven, set free, and made new by Jesus Christ.* Although you may think you are unable to forgive others or unable to forgive yourself, you must reach a point in your life where you are cleansed from the hurt of others and the stains of your own actions.

Some young people have asked, "Will this guilty feeling ever leave me?" First, you must determine if the guilt is justified at all. You have no reason to feel guilt over wounds if you were the victim rather than the villain. It is natural to feel ashamed, but through counseling and prayer, you can learn to overcome this.

The biggest obstacle to overcoming the shame and hurt is bitterness. You must learn to forgive and let go of the hatred, for it will only destroy you. Until you cut off bitterness at the root, the weeds of hatred will choke out any new life in you.

On the other hand, if you feel guilty because of the wounds you have inflicted on yourself by an immoral lifestyle, this can be used for good. Never run from a guilty conscience. It is the heart's way of cleansing you and bringing you to God. Instead, deal with it right away and allow healing to take place.

One wonderful trait about the God we love is that He not only forgives us completely, but *He forgets*: "As far as the east is from the west, / So far has He removed our transgressions from us" (Ps. 103:12). If God remembers your sin no more, why should you dwell on it further?

So then, a guilty conscience comes with the act of sin, but should not continue after confession. To *confess* is to "agree with." When you feel the same way about sin that God does (He hates it), then you will have no trouble putting it behind you. If you are having trouble putting a habit behind you, you probably like continuing that habit too much. Look at it through God's eyes, and its ugliness will drive you from it.

If ever there was a man who had to forgive himself of past actions, it was the apostle Paul. Called in the present to preach the gospel of Christ, he had to deal with the years of persecution and death he had personally brought to so many Christians in the past. His words were these: "One thing I do, forgetting those things which are behind and reaching forward to those things which are ahead." And then, *aiming high,* he concluded, "I press toward the goal for the prize of the upward call of God in Christ Jesus" (Phil. 3:13,14).

Don't try to drive forward while looking in the rearview mirror. It just won't work. I made the decision never to allow the past to handicap my future. The pain of the past is better left behind, and you, too, *can and must shake off the dust.*

10

LIVE LIFE AT THE PEAK

While you are growing and reaching toward an exciting future, you can make some changes now that will make the journey smoother. Just as the chameleon has the ability to change his color to deceive his predators, man has the ability to change his conduct to master his problems.

Twenty years after Edison's first incandescent bulb was developed, General Electric scientists asked, "By what changes can we improve it?"

In 1905, a new filament added 25 percent to the efficiency. In 1911, researchers changed the metal in the filament. New chemicals reduced size and blackening in 1912. In 1915, they redesigned the coil to prevent filament sag and eliminated the easily broken tip in 1919. The year 1925 brought bulb frosting to improve diffused light. In twenty years dedication to improvement brought progress and consumer benefits.

Each new invention was slow in coming, but each added a new dimension to the light bulb. Today some stores sell nothing but light bulbs—2,500 different types. It's been slow progress, but definitely worth the wait.

As you decide to *aim high*, what improvements can change make for you? After all, problems are simply challenges to improve.

You can make three changes now to help yourself live life to its fullest—*at the peak*.

1. A long look. Turn "clock watching" into "calendar watching."
2. A stable look. Feel your muscle, not your pulse.
3. A positive look. Think the best instead of the worst.

1. Watch the Calendar, Not the Clock.

The "clock watcher" frets with impatience. He demands immediate results. When success comes slowly, he moans, "What's the use? I quit!" *Quitters never win; winners never quit.*

Little values come quickly; big things take time. You can't grow an oak tree overnight. Growing an oak takes a "calendar watcher." In the same way, growing a good life takes time. You have decided to aim for this good life—a life lived at the peak of your capacity—and the realization of the decision will take time. Old habits and attitudes take time to be replaced with constructive and positive ones.

Now, stop watching the clock. Take the *long look* by putting the good life on your calendar. No, I'm not suggesting that you let today ride. Squeeze all you can out of today. Conquer every challenge that comes to you. But know that today is building toward the future—toward the rest of your calendar. Today, once it is completed, becomes a building block, never a stopping place.

A wise general, defeated in a skirmish, declared, "We lost a battle, but we will win the war!"

Every tennis player loses points but still can win sets. Every boxer takes blows but still can deliver the "knockout" punch. Every marriage has problems but still can produce the satisfactions of home. Every life has valleys as well as mountaintops but still can give fulfillment.

I saw an example of this on "Monday Night Football" as the team was down 0–24. Not willing to be defeated, the players played hard enough to come back and win, even though it meant going into overtime.

The "clock watchers" fail once and quit; the "calendar watchers" keep on and win.

You have begun the journey of helping yourself to a fulfilling life. Some days you will climb to a new peak; some days you will slip into a new chasm. The same is true of mountain climbing. No one walks the high ridge all the way. But you must keep climbing, or you will fall back to where you started. With patience, you will reach the peak.

Robert Bruce, the Scottish hero, had retreated to a mountain hut. Behind him were repeated defeats; before him unknown difficulties. All seemed lost. His cause appeared futile. Self-pity and discouragement plagued him.

Ready to quit the fight in surrender, Bruce happened to see a lone spider suspended on his web from a rafter. He watched the spider swing his web in a vain attempt to reach the next rafter. Again and again the Scottish general watched the tiny creature fail, only to try again and again. At last the exhausted spider hung motionless at the end of his web.

"How like my condition," mused Bruce.

The defeated general then decided, "If the spider tries again and succeeds, I will fight on. If the spider gives up, I, too, will admit defeat and surrender."

After a time of complete stillness, the spider moved again. This time he swung the web with success.

Bruce, true to his decision, gathered his scattered forces to fight again. Victory came! Freedom for his country brought honor to the memory of the man who marched on to the beat of triumph.

You may have followed the march of temporary defeat too long. Listen to the beat of a different drum. Listen to the charge of ultimate victory. When the "clock" strikes the hour of defeat, look to the "calendar." You can still win the war and overcome the enemies of your well-being.

> There was a man whose name was Jake,
> He wanted to quit when he made a mistake.
> But he saw his error,
> And ignored his terror,
> Who won the victory? Of course, it's Jake.

Does that sound silly? Maybe, but it does work. *Try the long look.*

Moses had the *long look,* for it is said,

> By faith Moses, when he became of age, refused to be called the son of Pharaoh's daughter, choosing rather to suffer affliction with the people of God than to enjoy the passing pleasures of sin, esteeming the reproach of Christ greater riches than the treasures in Egypt; for he looked to the reward (Heb. 11:24–26).

President Abraham Lincoln had the *long look.* He lost every election except his second bid for the presidency!

Take a new grip on your future. Abide by your decision to *aim high* and live life at the peak, to win with the *long look.* Don't wait. Make that decision now.

MY DECISION

To reach my goal to *live at my peak,* I have decided that time is on my side.

I reject shortsighted, fretful "clock watching."
I join the patient "calendar watchers."

Signed_____ Date_____

2. *Feel Your Muscle, Not Your Pulse.*

A "pulse feeler" lives with one finger on his wrist. Let anything happen and he takes his pulse. Every skip or jump in his heartbeat scares him. Fright increases the skips. He expects the worst. In fact, the true "pulse feeler" suffers even in good times, certain that bad times are coming soon.

Honestly, now, you have lived like this, haven't you? I know that your finger isn't really fastened to your wrist, but your mind is fixed on your troubles. You keep watching for an old symptom to return, for a new one to appear. If troubles come, your response is usually, "Just my luck!" You are really a "pulse feeler."

If you read a medical book, you convince yourself that you have all the symptoms of each sickness. How many times have you read an article and pointed out identical symptoms in your own body? How many times have you listened to the complaints of a friend and felt the same symptoms?

What should you do about this?

Take your finger off and allow your doctor to put his finger on your pulse. Let your physician decide if you have a real physical problem. If so, let him make the diagnosis and prescribe the treatment.

If the doctor finds no organic problem, forget your pulse. The fact that your heart *muscle* keeps beating is the important fact. Forget the skips and jumps. Excessive attention only amplifies the irregularity. After all, it's the muscle that really counts, not the pulse skips.

Begin the habit of feeling your *muscle, not your pulse.* Think how stable that muscle has been over the years, how it has developed and grown and become stronger. Picture in your mind the stormiest waves you have ever seen. The ocean floor remains stable through even the strongest of hurricanes.

Joshua needed the *stable look.* God commanded the way for the new leader to go, saying, "Do not turn from it to the right hand or to the left, that you may prosper wherever you go" (Josh. 1:7).

Jesus used the *stable look.* Of our Lord, it is recorded, "Who for the joy that was set before Him endured the cross, despising the shame, and has sat down at the right hand of the throne of God" (Heb. 12:2).

The sculptors of Mount Rushmore kept the *stable look* as each day for six and one-half years they transformed a mountain into the portraits of four American heroes.

The "pulse feeler" looks at the temporary and the passing. The "muscle feeler" looks at the permanent values. To the former, life is as fragile as the moment; to the latter, life has stability in the midst of change.

MY DECISION

I refuse to be a "pulse feeler" filled with fear because of the temporary. I determine to be a "muscle feeler" with my eyes steady on the permanent.

I will take the *stable look* at my life!

Signed_____ Date_____

3. Think the Best Instead of the Worst.

Have you ever witnessed the hulk weakened by hypnotic suggestion?

The weightlifter demonstrates his ability to lift a very heavy weight. He is then hypnotized. Under hypnosis he receives the suggestion that he will be unable to lift a much lighter weight. When the athlete tries to raise the lesser weight, he fails. Negative thought has robbed the "Samson" of his power.

Just so, much of human defeat results from thinking the worst instead of the best.

Take some examples:

"It is just my luck for something bad to happen."

"I never get the good breaks."

To keep thinking defeat is to keep experiencing defeat!

You experience defeat if you are uneasy about the future and depressed about the possibilities of your life. You experience defeat when you feel that others are against you or when you hesitate to start a project for fear of failure.

You can be a conqueror if you take pleasure in your accomplishments, feel good about the way the present is progressing, and are excited about the possibilities of the future.

The strange thing is that the words *defeat* and *conquer* really have similar meaning. The difference is in how they are applied. Will you defeat problems, or will you be defeated? Will you conquer challenges, or will they conquer you?

The book of Exodus tells us that the children of Israel followed a cloud through the desert. As they thirsted day after day, many thought of this constant cloud as useless for it never produced rain. The "useless" cloud fits the description of the age-old proverb: "Every cloud has a silver lining," for this cloud turned out to be the glory of God guiding and protecting them through the wilderness. God provided them with water, food, protection, and a plan for the future, always in a way the Israelites did not expect.

There is a positive aspect to every situation in life if you will only look for it. Often it is a valuable lesson learned the hard way but easily remembered for the days and years ahead. Thinking the best becomes a habit when you concentrate on the good. Thinking the best, and not the worst, renews your strength to bring the best into reality.

11

THE BEST IS YET TO COME

If there is not faith in the future, there will be no
power in the present.
—Dr. John Maxwell

Your attitude about the days ahead will regulate the
level of your enthusiasm today. You have already seen that
the future belongs to those who prepare today—educationally, spiritually, vocationally, and relationally. I hope
that this book has helped you to dream big dreams and,
more important, to establish balanced priorities. You can
face every day with the thought that the best is yet to come
in your life and in your future.

In your quest for excellence, you have seen the need for
short-term and long-term goals. You must have faith that
your immediate future and your eternity hold much
promise.

Since most graduates are more concerned about the
days ahead than the years ahead, let's look at a formula for
faith in the future:

But those who wait on the LORD
Shall renew their strength;
They shall *mount up* with wings like eagles,

They shall *run* and not be weary,
They shall *walk* and not faint (Isa. 40:31, emphasis added).

This verse promises strength for the days ahead. In fact, a close word study of the original Hebrew language implies that those who wait on the Lord shall "exchange" their strength. The Lord gives His power to the weak; He increases the strength of those who have no might. He helps people deal with life's oppression, opportunity, and occupations.

Mount Up

The image of the eagle is a powerful one to convey the idea of strength to soar above the storms of life, the *oppression* sometimes felt through adversity.

The first thing you should do when a storm hits is this: *don't panic.* Storms are inevitable in every life. Evaluate the storm and your possible methods of action. That is so much more effective than living in a state of panic and reacting to every storm, no matter what the size. Zig Ziglar says, "REACT = NEGATIVE. RESPOND = POSITIVE." As though anticipating our anxieties, God has placed the words *fear not* in the Bible 365 times, one for each day of the year.

The Scripture promises *strength*—"wings like eagles"— to endure the storm. Many naturalists believe that eagles actually like storms: a storm allows them to fly faster and higher.

There is also a biblical example of a *strategy* for the storm. Paul found himself sailing in the midst of a tempestuous storm: "And because we were exceedingly tempest-tossed, the next day they lightened the ship. On the third day we threw the ship's tackle overboard with our own hands" (Acts 27:18,19). All excess cargo was done away with.

The people on board that ship realized that either things or people would have to go. At this time in your life, you must understand that possessions have no lasting value—only people do.

As you evaluate the storm, notice the direction of the wind. If it is an unfavorable wind from the east, perhaps you can change your direction, even if temporarily, to turn it to a favorable wind. Be flexible in your plans. When a storm enters your life, don't give up on your goal. Just decide if you need to put it off for a while. For example, if someone you love is critically ill, then the care of that person might be your responsibility and priority at this time. But no situation is forever. You can ride out the storm with patience, endurance, and faith.

A lesson from the storm is that you should make every day count. Be sure that no week goes by without good memories to look back on. Don't let the days slip by into nothing, for they may be the only days you have. If you are eighteen now, you probably have 18,980 days left in your lifetime (based on a seventy-year life span). Then again you may have more or you may have less. Whatever your number of days on this earth, make them count to the fullest.

Paul and his fellow shipmates longed for a safe harbor. For you and me, the church can be that harbor. Dr. Robert Schuller reminds us, "A church can put strong wings on a weary heart." When you move away from home, *immediately* find a church home with a family who loves you and will minister to you.

THE BEST IS YET TO COME

Run

The Scripture also speaks of how you are to meet the opportunities life offers. The word *opportunity*, as we have already discussed, is a favorable wind blowing you toward the port of destination. The Scripture promises strength to *run* to the once-in-a-lifetime opportunities that come your way.

This is what you are preparing for now and why these next years are critical. But you have some opportunities today that will enable you to *run and not be weary* toward the opportunities of tomorrow. What you are becoming today will slam shut or open wide the doors of the future.

You have a chance today to develop an *honest mind,* a *pure heart,* and *seasoned speech.*

Honesty is the foundation of character; it is the basis upon which you can build a successful life. Develop the habit of being honest with yourself, honest before the all-knowing God, and honest in your dealings with others.

America has gone through a crisis of confidence. We have seen a lack of honesty in our political leaders, our financial leaders, and unfortunately, in some isolated cases, our spiritual leaders. *Ethics* is a word that has vanished from the vocabulary of too many people.

But some things never change, and the biblical writer many, many years ago clearly indicated the outcome for an honest person: "The truthful lip shall be established forever, / But a lying tongue is but for a moment" (Prov. 12:19). Honesty will earn you much more than a Scout merit badge; it will allow you to have a confident, rewarding future. The world is looking for men and women of good report who can be trusted.

To continue to be honest in mind, you must develop

purity of heart: "Blessed are the pure in heart, / For they shall see God" (Matt. 5:8). Biblical authors used the word *heart* to describe the very core of the personality. It involves the mind, the will, and the emotions.

This is the generation of "me." "What's in it for me?" is the ever-present question. Janet Jackson's popular song asked, "What have you done for me lately?" Many are preoccupied with the quest for pleasure, clothing, and status. In Florida the bumper stickers proclaim, "He who dies with the best tan wins." In other parts of the country we see, "He who dies with the most toys wins." But we know that the pure in heart shall live forever. And that is really winning. When the tan turns to skin cancer and the toys are repossessed, the pure in heart can still *aim high!*

Matthew 6:33 puts everything into perfect perspective: "Seek first the kingdom of God and His righteousness, and all these things shall be added to you." Author and pastor John Stott reminds us that:

> "extravagant and luxurious living; the hardheartedness which does not feel the colossal need of the world's underprivileged; the foolish fantasy that a person's life consists in the abundance of his possessions and the materialism that tethers our heart to this earth will cause our heart to lose its purity."

To be pure in heart, one must be grateful. You would do well to pray this prayer often: "Lord, You have given me so much. Please give me one thing more . . . *a grateful heart.*"

You will never outgrow your parents. They will only become more valuable friends as you grow older. Be thankful for the sacrifices they have made and the love they have shared with you. No matter how much or how little, understand that they gave all that they were capable of giving, both materially and emotionally. Shakespeare is quoted as saying, "How sharper than a serpent's tooth it is / To have a thankless child."

If you do not learn to be thankful, you will not be thanked. If you do not appreciate others, you will not be appreciated. This is part of having a sensitive spirit: sensitive to the moving of God's Spirit in your heart and sensitive to the needs of others before they ask.

The importance of guarding a pure heart is seen in these words: "For out of the abundance of the heart the mouth speaks" (Matt. 12:34). Your words can kill or give life. You hold that power in your hand or, should I say, in your tongue!

Develop a habit of looking for the good in others. Concentrate on finding something to praise instead of looking for a criticism or fault. Use your tongue for good to make others feel good about themselves.

"Getting together" doesn't have to mean "roasting all your friends who aren't present." Gossip, true or not, will damage a life, a reputation, a personality. The more you gossip, the greater chance you have of being gossiped about.

A woman once went to her minister to confess her sin of gossip. "What can I do to make it right?" she asked.

"Well," replied the minister, "take a sack of feathers up to the roof of the tallest building you can find. Open the sack and let the feathers fly into the wind. Then, proceed to go about the city picking up each feather and putting it back into the bag."

She laughingly responded, "You know that would never be possible."

"Yes," said the minister, "and neither is it possible to

gather in all the damage to lives and reputations that you have winded across your circle of acquaintances."

When you build up others, they are sure to build you up. Leave the demolition crew behind and join the construction team. The benefits are far greater!

Just making noise is not enough. Think! Don't let your tongue act more quickly than your brain. It has been said, "Think twice before you speak." The other side to that is that it will probably be twice as good, even though it may be only half as long! Author Leroy Brownlow has said, "Let your brain have an understanding before it has a tongue; and when stupidity seeks expression, close your lips a little tighter."

Getting your point across does not mean nagging. God gave two ears to listen and only one tongue to speak. James urges, "Let every man be swift to hear, slow to speak, slow to wrath; for the wrath of man does not produce the righteousness of God" (James 1:19,20). Keep your tongue from expressing anger. Others will be hurt by it. You will be hurt by it. Take the time to cool down and say what you have to say in a constructive manner.

As you *run* for opportunities, express self-control in your mind, heart, and tongue, for there is no greater feat. Peter the Great killed his own son in an outburst of fury. Though he overpowered many lands, he still considered himself to have failed. He declared, "I conquered an empire, but I was not able to conquer myself."

Walk

You will not devote the majority of your life to overcoming the valley of oppression or climbing the mountains of opportunity; you will spend most of your time on the plains of everyday *occupation*. Walking implies the necessary essentials of life.

It is important to have a job you enjoy, good friends, and a meaningful relationship with the Lord. These will keep you from being bored as you go through the daily routine of life. Even as you *aim high*, you will be required to take care of basic tasks. Many people fail at this and begin to look for outside diversions.

A marriage is a marriage forever. You do not look elsewhere to "spice it up." A job requires your full attention, but if you find yourself unhappy and therefore unable to give it your best, look for alternative projects rather than give in to poor performance. If you are in a position of leadership, take the time for recreation in your spirit. All giving and no receiving can leave you bankrupt. Be sure to plan time for refueling of the emotions as well as the mind. The human spirit is like a watch: it must be wound up. David felt this way when he cried, "He restores my soul" (Ps. 23:3).

You can have confidence in the promises of God; wait on the Lord and your strength will be renewed. Soaring like an eagle means to fly high above the earth. Ducks fly in flocks and geese fly in gaggles, but the eagle soars alone. Of course, there is danger in soaring high—*you might fall*. But then again, as you meander through life, *something might just fall on you*. You can go through life quacking and honking like the rest of the crowd, or you can dare to soar alone, to *aim high*.

The phrase "those who wait on the Lord" can also be translated "those who love the Lord." Not only is the best yet to come tomorrow, but also forever. As it is written, "Eye has not seen, nor ear heard, nor have entered into the heart of man the things which God has prepared for those who love Him" (1 Cor. 2:9). It is beyond our human capabilities to understand all that God has planned for us both here on the earth and in the glory and beauty of eternity.

If you are a child of God, you are on the winning side! You may not know what the future holds, but you know who holds the future. So don't be timid. *Aim high!* Live according to God's standard. Seek His will. Find strength through His Spirit. Then, one day when you look back on your life, you'll glow with the smile of success, knowing that you hit the target—you did it God's way.